PRAY LIKE A CATHOLIC

A Study of the Four Stages of Prayer According to St. Teresa of Avila

Susan Brinkmann, OCDS

PO Box 1173
Pottstown, PA 19464
www.CatholicLifeInstitute.org

NIHIL OBSTAT:
Robert A. Pesarchick, STD, STL, MA, M.Div

IMPRIMATUR:
Archbishop Charles J. Chaput, OFM Cap.
No. 00512, March 10, 2015

Catholic Life Institutes Press
PO Box 1173
Pottstown, PA 19464
www.CatholicLifeInstitute.org

Cover Design by IGD Graphic Design, www.image-gd.com

Pray Like a Catholic/ Susan Brinkmann – 1st ed.
ISBN-13: 978-1-7336724-1-2

"Prayer is simply being alone with Him, looking at Him, sharing His friendship, loving Him and allowing oneself to be loved...The important thing is not to think much but to love much..."

St. Teresa of Avila

CONTENTS

INTRODUCTION 1
FIRST STAGE OF PRAYER 9
SECOND STAGE OF PRAYER 27
THIRD STAGE OF PRAYER 49
FOURTH STAGE OF PRAYER 69
BIBLIOGRAPHY 83

INTRODUCTION

Catholic prayer has an image problem. In the modern quest for spirituality rather than religion, Eastern forms of prayer are promoted as rare and exotic while Christian prayer is presented as dull and old-fashioned.

Nothing could be further from the truth.

Authentic Catholic prayer is a supernatural adventure, a lifelong journey into the very heart of God. But most people don't see it this way at all. In fact, we're living at a time of great confusion about what exactly prayer is. Some folks see it as some kind of relaxation exercise where they use all kinds of techniques to "blank their minds." Others say it's just a time to ask God for favors, or to pray for our loved ones.

How about you? What do you think prayer is?
(Be honest!)

Let's ask that question with a little more specificity. What's the first thing that comes to your mind when you hear the words "Catholic prayer"?

____

____

____

____

____

____

Here's the Catechism's definition of prayer: "Prayer is the raising of one's mind and heart to God, or the requesting of good things from God" (No. 2559).

In other words, prayer is a dialogue with God. It's a time to "talk" to God.

Think about that for a moment! When you pray to God, how much time do you devote to actually listening to Him? Do you even know how to listen to Him?

That's just one of the many things this course will teach you to do. In fact, at the very end of the course, we're going to come back to this page and you'll be amazed at how different your answers will be!

So let's get started.

Perhaps the most amazing thing about authentic Catholic prayer is not so much its four glorious stages of prayer but the fact that this kind of prayer is not meant just for cloistered nuns and hermits. True Christian prayer is something we can all experience because of what it essentially is – a loving communion with God.

In "Some Aspects of Christian Meditation," Joseph Cardinal Ratzinger described Christian prayer as "a personal, intimate and profound dialogue between God and man."

Compared to Eastern forms of prayer such as transcendental meditation and centering prayer, Christian prayer "flees from impersonal techniques or from concentrating on oneself, which creates a kind of rut, imprisoning the person praying in a spiritual privatism," Cardinal Ratzinger writes. Instead of focusing on keeping the mind blank, the Christian focuses on keeping the heart and the soul open to the touch of its Beloved, in whatever form that touch might come – a word, a thought, a feeling.

In other words, anyone who can love God can go the distance in prayer. The basic requirements are love, perseverance, and docility to the Holy Spirit.

But we'll never get very far in prayer without the right attitude. Just like everywhere else in life, attitude makes all the difference. The wrong attitude can spoil everything – from our performance at work to how much fun we have on the family vacation. The same is true for prayer. If we approach it with the wrong attitude, we're going to get the wrong results. But what, exactly, is the right attitude?

In her book, *Welcome to Carmel,* Marilyn Zwick answers this question.

"A person who fails to develop the attitudes of patience, gentleness and perseverance in respect to his prayer will not only fail to develop these virtues in other areas of life, but will probably not last long as a person of prayer either."

Let's study each of these attitudes in depth.

Patience

The attitude of patience in prayer is not about learning how to wait for God's answers, but of learning how to be patient with ourselves. Anyone who embarks upon a serious prayer life has to realize that it's not always going to be a smooth ride. There will be days when prayer is as dry as old wood, when feelings of devotion just aren't there, when God and you seem to be light years apart.

It goes with the territory.

We need to be patient with ourselves, and with our reactions to these episodes of less-than-perfect prayer, especially because fluctuations in prayer are so much a part of the whole process of individual conversion. They teach us to depend on God rather than our own prayer skills. In the book, *Self-Abandonment to Divine Providence*, Father Jean-Pierre de Caussade explains this process:

"At certain times, God bestows and then takes away favors, in an almost continuous alternation, causing in the interior of souls perpetual variations. It is by continual changes and vicissitudes that God exercises souls in perfect submission of mind and heart . . . more or less like a wise and strong-minded mother who, in order to break a child's self-will and make him perfectly supple and docile, alternately gives and then deprives him of what he likes best. She caresses him, scolds him, flatters him, threatens him, and in less than an hour will make him do, or abstain from doing, a hundred different things. This is exactly the interior guidance God gives souls whom He wishes to train in pure and solid virtue."

Those who don't know or understand this principle, and who never developed patience with themselves, will almost certainly give up, never realizing that it's all perfectly normal.

Gentleness

God is gentle. He never forces us to do anything and respects our free will even more than we do. Even sinfulness shocks us more than Him, as we saw in Scripture when Jesus reacted so gently with the woman caught in adultery and Mary Magdalene who wept at His feet. If Jesus can be so gentle with us, why can't we?

The problem with most of us is that we expect too much from ourselves in prayer. We get upset over distractions, accidentally skipped prayers, even for not feeling as much fervor as we think we ought. God is not a "hair splitter" who fusses over every tiny detail of our prayer. Of the two persons engaged in prayer – ourselves and God – we're more likely to be the tedious taskmaster, not Him.

As a holy priest once instructed at a retreat, whenever we're tempted to be impatient and unkind with ourselves, think about those little stick-figure drawings children like to give to their parents. Regardless of how crude the drawings, what parent doesn't "ooh" and "ahh" over them as if they were an original Monet. This is exactly what God does with your less-than-perfect prayer! He sees the intention in your heart, and as long as you sincerely want to be with Him in prayer, that's what counts most in His eyes. He'll perfect your imperfections as time goes on.

In *Welcome to Carmel*, Zwick writes: "The reason most of us have difficulty with acquiring a gentle attitude is that we do not love ourselves enough. We have a difficult time accepting ourselves as we are and this attitude is contrary to gentleness."

It's also a sign of pride. We don't want to see how weak and inept we are. And so our pride prevents us from accepting our flaws and shortcomings with the same gentle acceptance that God does. If we try to be more like Him, we'll not only advance in our journey toward Him with much less anxiety, but this gentle attitude will inevitably spill over into other areas of our life, making us more accepting of our neighbor's faults as well.

Perseverance

This attitude is closely related to patience because a lack of patience limits our ability to persevere. When we hit those rough spots in the road of prayer, such as prolonged periods of dryness or distraction, perseverance is what will prevent us from becoming discouraged and giving up. These will be the times when we are the most vulnerable to Satan's number one temptation – to make us stop praying, or at least stop praying every day. Satan wants nothing more than to interrupt our daily communion with God by convincing us that we're getting nowhere.

If he can't get us to quit praying through discouragement or weariness, Satan might resort to the opposite tactic and incite us to do "great works for God" and thus become so busy we don't have time to pray.

Why is Satan so persistent about stopping us from praying? Because he knows it's the only way to God. The best way to counter his tactics is with a little of that good old-fashioned, teeth-gritting stubbornness otherwise known as persistence.

In her book, *The Way of Perfection*, St. Teresa of Avila called prayer the "royal road to heaven." She writes, "It is most important, all important, that souls should begin well by making an earnest and most determined resolve not to halt until they reach their goal (God), whatever may come, whatever may happen to them, however hard they may have to labor, whoever may complain of them, whether they reach their goal or die on the road . . ."

No matter how long our skies have been dark, we must never lose heart because God will always reward persevering souls, and come to our rescue sooner or later. St. Teresa assures us that God will see to it that "you will always find a few good people ready to help you" overcome or endure some temporary hardship in prayer. God will increase our desire not to stop praying by doubling up our courage and strengthening our resolve.

In short, our attitude is the fuel that will drive us along the road of prayer. A mixture of patience and perseverance will keep us moving forward, and just the right amount of gentleness will smooth many a rough spot along the "royal road to heaven."

FOR JOURNALING

Rank yourself in the three attitudes for prayer with the first being your strongest attitude and the third being the one in which you need the most work. Why did you rank yourself in this way? What steps might you take to improve in each attitude? Take this to prayer and ask the Lord for the grace to develop the right "fuel" to drive you along the road of prayer.

____

____

____

____

____

____

CHAPTER ONE

FIRST STAGE OF PRAYER
Vocal / Discursive Prayer

In her classic autobiography, *The Life of Teresa of Jesus*, the great mystical Doctor of the Church, St. Teresa of Avila, uses the analogy of watering a garden to describe this progression through the various stages of prayer.

The first way to water our garden, which is the most arduous, is to fill a bucket with water from a well and water the garden ourselves. This analogy represents the vocal/ discursive prayer with which we all start – a type of prayer that requires much effort, especially because in this early stage of our spiritual life, it is very difficult for us to keep our mind focused on spiritual matters. Our attachment to the world is still too strong, and we must struggle to put aside worldly affairs to concentrate, even for short periods of time, on God alone. When we do accomplish it, we are busy composing lengthy prayers, fatiguing our minds with lofty meditations, reciting litany after litany.

Even though vocal prayer is sometimes called the "beginning" stage of prayer, this doesn't mean it is inferior to other types of prayer. Remember, when Jesus was asked by the disciples to teach them to pray, it was the Our Father – a vocal prayer – that He taught them. When prayed properly, vocal prayer can launch one into higher forms of prayer.

But in the beginning of one's prayer life, this is the place where most newcomers to the spiritual life begin. Deeper forms of prayer are not yet within their grasp because they are still too attached to the world and its attractions to concentrate on God for long.

"...It will fatigue them to keep their senses recollected, which is a great labor because they have been accustomed to a life of distraction," writes St. Teresa of Avila in her autobiography, *The Life of Teresa of Jesus*.

Vocal Prayer

In order for vocal prayer to be efficacious, attention to God is required, not necessarily to every word spoken. St. Teresa gives us some practical advice on how to keep our mind on our prayers. She recommends that we practice praying the Our Father one phrase at a time, stopping between phrases to reflect on the words.

For instance, on the words "Our Father," we might pause to think about the many ways a father cares for his children, and then reflect on how God takes care of us in similar ways. When we say the words, "Who art in heaven," we might meditate on heaven and what it might be like to live with the blessed, free from our bodily restraints, and so on.

This is a way to pray vocally with great benefit. St. Teresa claims that while reciting vocal prayer, it is entirely possible for the Lord to grant a soul perfect contemplation. She writes, "In this way, His Majesty shows that He is listening to the person who is addressing Him, and that in His greatness, He is addressing her by suspending the understanding, putting a stop to all thought and, as we say, taking the words out of her mouth, so that even if she wishes to speak, she cannot do it."

St. Teresa tells the story of a distressed nun who came to her thinking she was unable to do anything but recite vocal prayers. She was badly bothered by distractions during her prayer time and would spend hours reciting the Our Father just a few times to keep her mind focused on God. Upon questioning this sister, Teresa learned that while she was reciting those few Our Fathers, "she was experiencing pure contemplation." Her virtue and manner of life revealed she was indeed receiving great favors from God in prayer – without realizing it!

But what about prayer that is longer than an Our Father or two, such as the rosary? Aren't our minds bound to wander after we've been praying for a while?

Of course! For this reason, Father Gabriel tells us that we shouldn't expect to grasp every word of lengthier vocal prayer, only to keep ourselves in the presence of God while reciting them. A general thought about the meaning of the words, or a simple glance at the God to whom we are addressing our prayer, might be sufficient.

Another common problem with vocal prayer is excessive multiplication of prayers. Some people get into a set habit of repeating litany after litany, devotion upon devotion, prayer after prayer, which may leave little or no time for God to get a word in edgewise. This type of prayer can also cause monotony which makes it much too easy to fall into the habit of rattling off words without considering the meaning behind them.

To avoid this, interject a pause now and again in your prayers to bring your mind back to the words.

"We are under the obligation of trying to pray attentively," St. Teresa tells us in *The Way of Perfection.* Notice the word she uses – *trying.*

Let's face it, we're only human. There will be days when we can't string together two good thoughts during an entire rosary. These are the times when we can appreciate why St. Teresa placed such a great emphasis on the need to develop the virtue of perseverance in our prayer lives. No matter what, we must keep faithful to our daily prayer, regardless of how good or bad it might be.

If today we do not pray well, perhaps tomorrow we will do better. This must be our attitude with any kind of prayer, vocal or contemplative, because it's the resolute soul who will ultimately win the favor of God. As St. Teresa tells us, "The devil is very much afraid of resolute souls, knowing by experience that they inflict great injury upon him." Why? Because "a resolute person fights more courageously. He knows that, come what may, he must not retreat."

Let's take a look at another form of discursive prayer – meditation.

Meditation

The purpose of Christian prayer is to enter into dialogue with God and to increase our love for Him. This is what distinguishes Christian meditation from that of other faiths.

For instance, many Eastern forms of meditation such as Transcendental Meditation and Centering Prayer focus on the self rather than on God, with the primary goal being to emptying the mind. Although Catholic meditative practices also seek to quiet the intellect, the principle aim is to acquire a loving knowledge of God.

"Meditation is above all a quest," says *The Catechism of the Catholic Church*. "The mind seeks to understand the why and how of the Christian life, in order to adhere and respond to what the Lord is asking" (No. 2705).

The mind, then, plays an important role in authentic Christian contemplation and is definitely not something we want to "empty."

"Meditation engages thought, imagination, emotion and desire. This mobilization of faculties is necessary in order to deepen our convictions of faith, prompt the conversion of our heart, and strengthen our will to follow Christ" (No. 2708).

The Catechism teaches us that the overall aim of Christian prayer is always to bring us to the knowledge of the love of the Lord Jesus, and to union with Him.

In other words, we employ our minds only in so far as they awaken our hearts to love.

Before beginning meditation, it is important to understand how the human mind operates in order to better control it during prayer. According to Father Benedict Groeschel, a Franciscan Friar of the Renewal and professor of psychology, there are two primary modes in which our mind operates – the beta and the alpha mode. He discusses both in his book, *Listening at Prayer*.

The beta mode is more active and precise while the alpha mode is more intuitive and contemplative. Our mind is in beta mode when we are engaged in everyday activities such as working or studying. We're in alpha mode when we're listening to music or enjoying the company of loved ones because this mode is more relaxed and receptive. In alpha mode, we focus on the whole picture without dissecting its many parts, whereas in beta mode, we examine every little detail.

For instance, we can dissect the attributes of God in beta mode, or we can contemplate the overall mystery and intrigue of our Creator in alpha mode. Obviously, the latter mind-set is more conducive to increasing our love and reverence for God.

This is why, when we begin prayer, especially meditative or mental prayer, it is important to learn how to "switch modes" because this is something we have some control over.

One way to achieve this switch is to recite a prayer for someone you know, then sit back and reflect on your intention. In practice, we may recite a Hail Mary for a sick relative, and then meditate on offering this person into Our Lady's care.

This same approach can be applied to reading Scripture. In beta mode, we read the verse. In alpha mode, we meditate on the verse or story from the gospel, turning it over in our minds, picturing the situation, perhaps feeling the accompanying emotions.

When we pray the Our Father slowly, reflecting on each word, this is another example of how we teach ourselves to switch from beta to alpha mode. First we say the words, then we envision the meaning.

Over time, and with sustained practice, we can actually learn to turn our entire lives into a prayer by applying the alpha mode to the way we think during the day!

Father Groeschel gives a good example of how this can be done. He uses the verse, "Come, let us adore Him," and applies it to the different circumstances of a day.

For instance, while shopping, we see racks full of beautiful items and reflect on the providence of God who has provided for our every need. "Come, let us adore Him!"

An old woman shuffles past us toward the door, her eyes downcast with sorrow. We open the door and wish her a good day, which brings a bright smile to her face. "Come, let us adore Him!"

Reflect on a verse throughout the day in this way helps us to switch from a busy mindset to a more contemplative one, and enables us to see a whole different dimension in the world around us, a dimension where God is wholly present.

As we grow in our spiritual lives, we will hopefully come to the point where words will no longer be necessary in order to meditate. We will be content to sit in silence with our inner gaze fixed on the Lord, ready to hear Him speak in the depths of our soul.

There are various methods of meditation that can be employed, such as the practice of *Lectio Divina* which involves a prayerful meditation of the Scriptures. Meditation is also integral in the Spiritual Exercises of St. Ignatius of Loyola. The Rosary is another excellent method because it leads us into meditation on major events in the life of Christ. The Jesus Prayer is also popular and consists of saying a short prayer such as "Lord Jesus Christ, Son of God, have mercy on me a sinner" while focusing both mind and heart on Jesus.

All of these methods are good, but they are only a guide to show us the way into meditative prayer.

St. Francis de Sales gave good advice about this type of mental/meditative prayer when he said we should behave like a bee that settles on a flower as long as it finds honey in it, and then moves to the next one. When you cease to draw inspiration from a thought and your mind begins to wander, return to your vocal prayer or other source of meditation.

The next form of discursive prayer that we will explore is perhaps the most important of all – mental prayer.

Mental Prayer

This is such an incredibly simple kind of prayer that the best way to learn about it is to try it.

Take a moment now to imagine what it would be like if Jesus showed up on your doorstep. What would He look like standing on your stoop? Perhaps he would be dressed like He was when He appeared after the resurrection, in a plain white tunic that reaches to the floor and a simple corded belt around his waist. His hair would be long and brown and his eyes would be remarkably easy to look into, so gentle and clear and full of quiet joy.

Of course you would invite Him inside and probably seat Him in your favorite chair. He'd motion for you to come and sit by his feet, then ever so gently ask, "So how are you? What's been going on in your life? Is there anything you need me to do for you?"

Close your eyes, and imagine yourself in this scene. How would you answer His questions? What would you say if you had the Son of God all to yourself, with Him ready and willing to grant you whatever help you need?

However you answer that question is not important. What really matters is what you're doing when you attempt to answer it – engaging in mental prayer.

Yes, it's that simple, that easy.

And yet spiritual masters have long counseled the faithful that 30 minutes a day of this kind of prayer can do more for one's spiritual life than two theology degrees and a whole library of spiritual books.

"The person who is fully determined to make a half hour's mental prayer every morning, cost what it may, has already traveled half his journey," St. Teresa of Avila says.

Why? Because as simple as this prayer is, for many people, it's the most difficult to practice for a variety of reasons. Some find it difficult to pray without the "props" of vocal prayer. Others find it too difficult to sustain for long before being assailed by distractions. Then there are those who feel unworthy of such intimate one-on-one contact with God. Heart-to-heart is just too close for comfort!

Thankfully, God already knows what's preventing us from having this kind of intimate contact with Him and He's more than willing to grant us the grace to rise above these challenges. All we need to do is ask for His help, and then be open to receiving it.

One of the most important ways to open ourselves to receiving this grace is to commit some time every day to the practice of mental prayer. Start out with five minutes, then try for 10 or 15. No matter how many distractions we encounter, or how "poorly" it seems to be going, stick to it. In time, God will reward your efforts.

For those whose imaginations need some help, try using a picture of Jesus to form an appealing image of Him in the mind.

Others can employ a similar practice as we did in the beginning of this lesson by imagining the Lord sitting next to you, listening to all you have to say.

But be careful not to allow any strain or struggle into this practice.

"This friendly conversation will not be much thinking but much loving," St. Teresa teaches. "Not a torrent of words, much less a strained prepared speech, but rather a relaxed conversation with moments of silence as there must be between friends."

Why not start out by telling the Lord how you feel about this kind of prayer. You might say, "Lord, this feels awkward!" or "I can't think of what to say!" The more honest and heartfelt, the better.

The important thing to remember is that in order to have such a casual heart-to-heart exchange with God in prayer, technique means nothing. What really matters is love.

This love moves us to spend time alone with God not for what we get out of it, but for what we can put into it. We shouldn't go to mental prayer because it makes us feel good or because we want a spiritual experience. We should go to it because we want to be open to God's love and allow Him to take over our lives.

In the book *Soul of the Apostolate,* Dom Jean-Baptiste Chautard, OCSO writes: "We need to be thoroughly convinced of the fact that all God asks of us, in this conversation, is good will. A soul pestered by distractions, who patiently comes back each day, like a good child, to talk with God, is making first-rate mental prayer. God supplies all our deficiencies."

But how do we acquire such deep and thoughtful prayer habits? Our Church's spiritual masters have given us plenty of advice on how to accomplish this.

St. Teresa of Avila tells us that we must set aside a specific time for prayer every day and be faithful to this time no matter what. Pick a time that does not cause you to shirk the duties of your state in life, but will be the least likely to bring distractions and other interruptions by the affairs of life.

Second, make the commitment to give that time exclusively to God. If we don't do this, our prayer tends to be half-hearted. In his book, *Temptation and Discernment*, Father Segundo Galilea, OCD, calls this "prayer undertaken only halfway... We have one foot in prayer and the other outside."

Father Dom Chautard gives several useful tips a person can employ to help foster the practice of mental prayer:

1. Use a book such as the Bible, read a few lines, then pause in between to allow the words to draw out some affection or feeling of contrition.
2. Say a vocal prayer, such as the Our Father, very slowly, pausing to ponder more deeply each word or phrase.

3. When prayer is completely dry or hopelessly riddled with distractions, “abandon yourself generously to this suffering, without anxiety, and without making any effort to avoid it.” Then unite this barren prayer with some aspect of Jesus’ suffering and death.

4. Examine your conscience. “Admit your defects, passions, weaknesses, infirmities, helplessness, misery, nothingness. ... This kind of prayer is very free and unhampered and admits all kinds of affections.”

5. Imagine yourself standing before God on the day of your judgment. “What would you wish to have done? How would you have wanted to live?”

6. Imagine yourself in the Presence of Jesus in the Blessed Sacrament, and end by making an act of spiritual communion.

7. Put yourself in the presence of God “without making any other distinct thought. ...Relax in this simple awareness of God’s presence.”

8. If we persevere in the practice of vocal and discursive prayer, we may soon find ourselves on the threshold of the second stage of prayer – contemplation.

However, the transition between the first and second stage of prayer is very subtle and unless one is educated in the ways of prayer, it’s easy to misunderstand the new longings that arise during prayer, thinking they are merely daydreams rather than what they truly are – the signs of advancing prayer.

PITFALLS IN PRAYER

Distractions

This is the first of many pitfalls that you will be learning about in this course. Distractions are the most common of all pitfalls because they plague everyone from sinner to saint.

Yes, even the saints suffered from distractions. Teresa of Avila, who is the Church's foremost authority on prayer, once described the way her imagination wandered during prayer as being "like a madwoman running through the house." She completely understood souls whose "minds are so scattered they are like wild horses no one can stop. Now they're running here, now there, always restless." She readily admits in her *Way of Perfection*, "I suffered many years from this trial – and it is a very great one – of not being able to quiet the mind in anything."

So how do we deal with distractions?

Father Gabriel of St. Mary Magdalen suggests in *Divine Intimacy* that we take a few precautions that can help to prevent distractions. First, "make a firm decision of the will to put aside everything when you come to prayer – all cares and preoccupations with human things, and concentrate all the powers of the soul on God alone."

Believe it or not, few of us do this the way we ought. The time for prayer must be considered sacred. We should withdraw into a place of solitude where we can totally avoid people, business, etc. This time must belong exclusively to God.

But most of don't do this – at least not until we become more disciplined. It's hard to pray with the TV blaring from the other room or while trying to maneuver the expressway at rush hour. No wonder we're distracted!

Cutting down on the possibility for distraction is an important first step in coming to terms with this annoying condition.

Another way is to take notice of exactly what distracts you at prayer. You might be surprised to discover that it's mostly unnecessary things, or business we can tend to when we're finished praying.

Distractions such as these can be conquered simply by keeping a notepad and pen nearby where you can write them down, then forget about them until a more appropriate time.

Another way to avoid distractions is to not try to change your mood to suit your prayer – this only gives you more reason to keep dwelling upon whatever is upsetting you rather than praying.

Instead, let your prayer fit your mood. If you're happy, thank God for every little thing that's making you joyful. Sing songs to Him in your heart and/or meditate on the joyful mysteries of the rosary. If you're sad, sit beside Jesus and tell Him your troubles. Perhaps walk with Him along the road to Calvary, adding your troubles to the weight of His cross, then helping Him to carry it.

However you attempt to avoid distractions, they will still come to some degree or another, which is why the most important thing to do about them is to learn how to avoid getting upset over them. They're a part of our human condition and no matter how advanced we are in our spiritual life, they will always plague us.

As Teresa explains, "This (mental) restlessness is either caused by the soul's nature or permitted by God." In either case, anxiety is quite useless and only makes everything worse.

Father J. P. de Caussade, S.J., one of the Church's most distinguished spiritual directors, once wrote about how to handle distractions, disturbing thoughts and other spiritual weaknesses in *Self-Abandonment to Divine Providence.*

"First, never cling to them voluntarily; second, neither endure nor resist them with violent effort since this merely strengthens them. Allow them to drop as a stone drops into water . . ." In other words, *ignore them.* The moment we realize we've been daydreaming, calmly return our attention to God, even if we have to do this a hundred times in a half-hour of prayer.

This might take some practice at first because our instinct is to get upset. But even if we do, the additional advice of St. Francis de Sales can help. "Neither be troubled that you are troubled, nor be anxious that you are anxious, nor be disturbed that you are disturbed, but turn naturally to God in sweet and peaceful humility, going so far as to thank Him that He has not allowed you to commit greater faults."

The important thing is to "be determined to be determined" to pray, St. Teresa tells us. Let nothing stand in our way, not even ourselves! The object is to stick to our prayer no matter what and never stop asking the Holy Spirit to help us pray as we ought. If we humbly ask for His assistance, He will surely come to our aid. Perhaps not today, or even tomorrow, but eventually He will.

In conclusion, Teresa advises, "Little by little, accustom the soul with coaxing and skill not to grow discouraged. ..."

We must pray every day for a certain prescribed time and let nothing stop us – not dryness, fatigue or distractions. As this great saint told us five hundred years ago, "I assure you, that if with care you grow accustomed to what I have said, your gain will be so great that even if I wanted to explain this to you, I wouldn't know how."

In the next chapter, we will learn about these signs of advancing prayer and how to be receptive to God's gift of the second stage of prayer.

FOR JOURNALING

Take time this week to practice the three forms of prayer. For example, for vocal prayer, practice praying the Our Father by focusing on one phrase at a time. For meditation, use Fr. Groeschel's suggestions. Mental prayer can be just a few minutes spent in a loving heart-to-heart conversation with Jesus.

Make note of when and where you choose to pray – in bed before the family awakes in the morning; in the evening before bed. Is this the best place or time to give your full attention to God?

What kind of distractions did you have during your prayer time? Make a list of the things you were thinking about – were they important or just wandering thoughts? Take note of how you responded to them. Did you feel annoyed with yourself?

Make a note of any thoughts or inspirations you had during this time. Be careful not to fall into the trap of "grading yourself" on how well you did in prayer. God always ranks the intention higher than the action so pay more attention to what's in your heart than what's in your head.

CHAPTER TWO

SECOND STAGE OF PRAYER
Infused Contemplation

The second way to water our garden is to use a water wheel to draw the water up, which requires less effort on our part and yields more water.

One of the clearest signs that we have crossed the threshold from the first to the second stage of prayer is when we stop relating to God as "the man upstairs" and realize that He is within us and is as close to us as our very breath. We know that we've made this new connection when this deepening awareness of God within causes our prayer time to "leak" into the rest of our lives. Suddenly, we find ourselves talking to Him all day long. He is not just our "prayer God" anymore. Now He's become a true friend and constant companion.

As simple as it might sound, the practice of the presence of God represents a turning point in our prayer life. It is the mark that we are maturing in our faith and moving toward the next stage of prayer.

Let's take a closer look at this practice.

The Practice of the Presence of God

Brother Lawrence of the Resurrection considered himself to be clumsy and inept and deserving of no higher work than making soup in the kitchen of a Carmelite monastery and yet it was to him that God revealed the secrets of His Kingdom here on earth. The small collection of letters written three hundred years ago by this inconspicuous lay brother became one of the Church's most beloved classics, *The Practice of the Presence of God.*

As Brother Lawrence explains, when Jesus said, "The Kingdom of God is within you," He meant exactly that. God dwells in each one of us. This is a truth we learn about in grade school and yet very few people take seriously.

But once we come to a practical understanding of it – that God really is present within each of us at every moment of every day – feeling, thinking, hearing, seeing everything right along with us – and we become *aware* of this Presence within ourselves – a whole new dimension of life opens up. We suddenly become more conscious of living not only as a physical being, but as a spiritual being as well. Living with God in this way becomes the ultimate form of existence, the optimal lifestyle. Nothing can surpass it because His Presence is pure joy, even in the worst moments, the most severe trials, and it quickly becomes the greatest treasure of our life. In fact, we can become so intimately associated with Him that we no longer feel like ourselves without Him.

These are among the secrets God revealed to Brother Lawrence. "God alone is capable of revealing Himself as He really is," he wrote. "Neither skill or knowledge is needed to go to Him. All we have to do is recognize God as being intimately present within us. Then we may speak directly to

Him every time we need to ask for help or to know His will in moments of uncertainty, etc."

The practice of the Presence of God does not depend so much on changing our activities as it does on doing them for God rather than for ourselves. For most of us, this will require some work.

"To accomplish this, it is necessary for the heart to be emptied of everything that will offend God," Brother Lawrence wrote. "He wants to possess your heart completely. Before any work can be done in your soul, God must be totally in control."

This is part of a spiritual process that takes a lifetime, and it's one none of us can escape.

"When we begin our Christian walk, we must remember that we've been living in the world, subject to all sorts of misery, accidents and poor dispositions within," Brother Lawrence writes. "The Lord will cleanse and humble us in order to make us more like Christ. As we go through the cleansing process, we grow closer to God" and become more and more accustomed to His Presence within us.

This familiarity can come about only through the practice of a continual awareness of God's Presence by talking with Him throughout the day. Brother Lawrence often spoke very simply and frankly to God during the day to ask for help as he needed it and God never failed to respond.

"During my work, I would always continue to speak to the Lord as though He were right with me," he wrote.

This was especially comforting to him when he had to do something stressful. He would simply call on his Friend and say, "I'm capable of nothing without you." Help would be there in an instant, and usually in much greater proportions than he would ever dare to ask.

"When I am with Him, nothing frightens me," Brother Lawrence wrote, which is why he strove to never lose sight of God no matter where he was or what he was doing.

But this takes practice. "Stay as close as possible to God, doing, saying and thinking nothing that might displease Him. The soul's eyes must be kept on God, particularly when something is being done in the outside world."

This can be either a clear and distinct knowledge of God or just a general loving remembrance of Him in the midst of activity. "Since much time and effort are needed to perfect this practice, one should not be discouraged by failure." One should faithfully practice God's presence every day, but "gently, humbly and lovingly, without giving way to anxiety or problems."

A person might want to use short phrases to recall God's presence, such as "Jesus, be with me" or even just a simple, "Hi, Lord!" After awhile, these words won't be necessary because the habit of staying in tune with God will grown into a kind of wordless sharing of everything we encounter during the day from answering a phone call at work to sharing a moment of relaxation after dinner. Realizing God's Presence will slowly become a habit, and eventually a way of life.

And what a way of life it is to abide constantly in the embrace of the Author of Life and the Source of all joy and beauty! Brother Lawrence lived in a state of almost constant joy, a happiness that was sometimes so overwhelming he had to struggle to keep it hidden from others.

But don't be fooled into thinking this practice will prevent us from being fully engaged in life. Brother Lawrence was known to be always full of energy and vitality, even in the kitchen where he so often worked. He often did the work of two people, yet never seemed stressed or hurried. Instead, he gave his full attention to each chore, working neither slowly nor swiftly and always dwelling in calmness of soul and an unalterable peace. So constant was the inner joy of his soul that he would often tell the Lord that he felt deceived because his Christian walk had thus far been so pleasant and not filled with the kind of suffering he expected.

As we practice living this most fundamental truth of our faith, "the soul discovers in God a beauty infinitely surpassing not only that of bodies that we see on earth, but even that of the angels," Brother Lawrence promises.

Faith is enlarged, the will is strengthened, love becomes a slow steady fire in the soul and we are alive now, no longer as mere humans, but as children in the Kingdom of God.

The Beginnings of Infused Contemplation

As simple as it may seem, this prayerful awareness of the indwelling God is the beginning of contemplative prayer and naturally leads into a kind of prayer known as the *prayer of recollection.*

Also known as *acquired recollection* or *acquired contemplation,* the soul "gathers together all its faculties and enters within itself to be with its God." One may choose to just sit in quiet awareness of God, or to use vocal prayer, but the mind will remain recollected in God. It is not a silencing of the faculties, but is an "enclosing of the faculties within itself," Teresa explains. This is not yet a supernatural state but depends upon our will, which means it's still an acquired rather than a mystical or infused grade of prayer.

This prayer "consists in the realization of this great truth: God is in me, my soul is His temple; I recollect myself in the intimacy of this temple to adore Him, love Him, and unite myself to Him," explains Father Gabriel of St. Mary Magdalen.

Just as we learned in the practice of the presence of God, the soul who has the sense of the presence of God within it possesses one of the most efficacious means of making prayer.

"Do you believe," says St. Teresa of Jesus, "that it is of little importance for a soul who is easily distracted, to understand this truth [that God is in it] and to know that, in order to speak with its heavenly Father and to enjoy His company it does not have to go up to heaven or even to raise its voice? No matter how softly it speaks, He always hears it, because He is so near. It does not need wings to go to contemplate Him in itself," she writes.

In this form of prayer, there is no struggle to find the right prayer or form the perfect plea. When it comes to contemplative prayer, our main task is to sit in the presence of God and receive whatever He wants to give.

As simple as it sounds, many of us find this very difficult to do. Why?

Because sitting quietly and thinking about God too often feels like we're wasting time, especially if we're accustomed to a more structured prayer life where we're relying on the recitation of certain prayers for part of the time or perhaps some spiritual reading. Even when the urge to "step out of the box" is strong, many of us still fight the urge to be still, not realizing these desires might be coming from the Holy Spirit who is prompting us to follow Him into newer realms of encountering God. In this realm, prayer is simpler and might consist of short loving colloquies, quiet meditations interspersed with spiritual reading, or just plain silence.

The bottom line is that as we approach the second stage of prayer, it's okay to lose our taste for long litanies and extensive vocal prayers. If we want to just sit and "be" with God rather than meditating or saying our usual prayers, go ahead and try it.

But be careful to resist the urge to go overboard in the opposite direction. For instance, some respond to this need for silence by trying to "blank the mind" and void it of any thoughts. These techniques are derived from Eastern forms of meditation which are actually mental exercises aimed at achieving altered states of consciousness. They are not like Christian meditative practices which are aimed at producing a loving dialogue between the soul and God.

Christian contemplative prayer is all about love, not techniques, and people can expect to advance in this type of prayer in direct proportion to their generosity in embracing the Gospel of Jesus Christ.

As Peggy Wilkinson defines, contemplation is "a loving gaze upon God with the eyes of the soul."

This love comes about naturally as we progress toward the next stage of prayer. By now, we have grasped the concept of a loving God within us and have begun to practice it daily. As we do so, God becomes an ever-closer companion and confidant. Our love for Him deepens until we find ourselves unwilling to do anything to displease Him. Life without Him eventually becomes unthinkable. These sentiments eventually morph into yet another characteristic of contemplative prayer, the desire for union with God.

An ever deepening love for God results in ever higher degrees of contemplation, but in order to love Him more, we must persevere in both our prayer life and in our commitment to the Gospel.

If we do so, our *prayer of recollection* will begin to deepen into what is known as the *prayer of infused contemplation* which is more profound and powerful. This inner stillness may last anywhere from a few seconds to several minutes and is usually so subtle at first we can easily mistake it for daydreaming or "zoning out."

But it's not. These are the first touches of infused contemplation.

This striving for union with God is a spiritual version of the yearning of lovers to consummate their love. These yearnings will eventually lead into higher degrees of contemplative prayer. These degrees are commonly called "infused" because their origin is not from us, but from God.

"Infused contemplation is a divinely given, general, non-conceptual loving awareness of God," explains Fr. Dubay. "There are no images, no concepts, no ideas, no visions. Sometimes this awareness of God takes the form of loving attention, sometimes a dry desire, sometimes of a strong thirsting. None of these experiences are the result of reading or reasoning – they are given and received.

"The infusion is serene, purifying. It can be delicate and brief or in advanced stages, burning, powerful, absorbing, prolonged. Always it is transformative of the person; usually imperceptibly and gradually but on some occasions obvious and suddenly."

Especially in these first experiences of infused prayer, "the beginner needs to be well instructed or he is likely to miss what is given at this point, so gentle and delicate it is," writes Fr. Dubay. "Being such, they can be easily stifled by unwise efforts to pray actively."

This is because in infused prayer, the Lord gradually takes over the will, then the intellect and imagination. St. Teresa calls this "suspension of the faculties . . ." which means God is beginning to bypass the senses in prayer and speaks directly to the soul.

And all the while, the Lord is gradually enlarging the soul to receive an even more powerful form of mystical prayer known as the *prayer of quiet.*

In this prayer, the Lord completely captures the will and unites it with His own, sometimes suspending the faculties so completely a person is aware of nothing around them. Whole blocks of time, 10 to 20 minutes, may simply "disappear" without one knowing or remembering anything about what took place. This is accompanied by a deep peace, not of human origin that penetrates the soul and sometimes lingers for days afterward. There is no doubt in our minds that we have encountered God, although we find the experience almost impossible to describe.

In spite of how brief is this absorption in God, the soul is never able to forget it. For the rest of our lives, we will remember the exact time and place that it occurred.

The important thing to remember during this stage of prayer is that "This quiet and recollection – this little spark – if it proceeds from the Spirit of God and is not a pleasure bestowed on us by the devil or sought by ourselves, is not a thing that can be acquired," St. Teresa writes. "This spark is given to the soul by God as a sign or pledge that He is already choosing it for great things if it will prepare itself to receive them."

She goes on to say: "We can no more control this prayer than make the day break, or stop night from falling. It is supernatural (infused) and something we cannot acquire."

How do we prepare ourselves to receive such an exquisite gift?

First, be open to the gift! When the first sign of these favors appears, put aside all discursive prayer and let the Lord have His way.

"What the soul has to do at these seasons of quiet is merely to go softly and make no 'noise'," Teresa says. By "noise" she means trying to think up all kinds of loving words to say.

Instead, just be still and let it happen.

Believe it or not, most people will advance to this second stage of prayer, and those who wish to go further should follow the three conditions for growth laid out by St. Teresa:

1. Never give up the habitual practice of prayer, whether it be full of consolation or as dry as the desert.

2. Detach from everything. "If there is no lessening of selfish clinging, there is no growth in prayer," says Fr. Dubay. Otherwise, we will remain too smothered by the cares and riches and pleasures of life.

3. Seek greater solitude. While being careful never to forsake our duties in life, we must seek to be more like Jesus who often went off by Himself to be alone with the Father in prayer.

Once the soul has begun to receive these favors, it may think it has found heaven on earth. But as we will discover in the third stage of prayer, this is just the beginning of what God has ready for those who love Him.

Now let's take a closer look at the signs of advancing prayer.

Signs of Advancing Prayer

A prayer technique might be able to bring us to Nirvana in three easy steps, but authentic prayer isn't about entering a state of perfect peace – it's about entering into communion with the Perfect. There's just no substitute for a genuine experience of union with the All Holy and Triune God.

But no one can come near such a perfect and pure God without first undergoing a period of purification. This is the cross that accompanies all true Christian prayer. The more purified we become of sinful inclinations and inordinate attachments, the closer we can come to God in prayer. This process is sometimes painful, frequently frustrating, and always humiliating.

But it works.

"Advancing communion with God does not happen in isolation from the rest of life," writers Father Thomas Dubay, SM. "One's whole behavior pattern is being transformed as the prayer deepens. So true is this that if humility, patience, temperance, chastity, and love of neighbor are not growing, neither is prayer growing. Hence, contemplation is not simply a pious occupation in the chapel or in some other solitude."

Trying to conform ourselves to Christ in a secular and pluralistic society as our own brings plenty of purification to the average Christian. One can't even stand in line at the supermarket without being bombarded with magazines covered with impure images and stories about Hollywood's latest scandal. Our belief system is regularly maligned by the cultural and political elites; our families are threatened; our children slaughtered in the womb. Our efforts to respond in a Christ-like fashion to these grave injustices and ever-creeping immoralities is trial enough for anyone!

It's all part and parcel of the kind of purification Christians will go through as we make our way through life. However, if we're faithful to our daily prayer and do the best we can to overcome our faults, God may begin favoring us with the beginnings of infused prayer long before we've been sufficiently purified.

Consider the literal meaning of the word infused – it means *to pour in*. The more we "get empty" the more room we make for the coming infusion of divine prayer.

These initial infusions are usually so subtle they completely escape us, Dubay writes, "The reality is so unimposing that one who lacks instruction can fail to appreciate exactly what is taking place. Initial infused prayer is so ordinary and unspectacular in the early stages that many fail to recognize it for what it is. Yet with generous people, that is, with those who try to live the whole Gospel wholeheartedly and who engage in an earnest prayer life, it is common."

However, our inclination is to over-complicate things. Surely infused contemplation, this mysterious state of the saints, is something quite unforgettable, right? Well, not exactly, at least not in the early stages. In the beginning, it's really rather ordinary. As St. Teresa of Avila describes, it's simply "a being alone with the God who loves us."

It may start as a subtle urge to go off somewhere alone and pray. Or we may find ourselves thinking about God while occupied during the day much like a person would briefly recall a loved one. Perhaps we've begun to develop the practice of the presence of God within us and are sharing more and more of our everyday life with Him.

Anyone who has experienced these examples can say they are hardly spectacular experiences. In fact, they are so unspectacular we can easily miss them!

Spectacular or not, these are the signs of advancing prayer, namely that of infused prayer. "Because it could not be more simple, the very simplicity is part of the problem of explanation," Dubay writes.

In order to help us recognize these initial experiences, Father Dubay lists some of the basic elements of this more advanced form of prayer:

- One experiences God's presence in either a peaceful, general, loving attention, or as a "dry reaching out for Him."
- There is a great deal of fluctuation in the intensity of these feelings. Sometimes they're felt very powerfully, other times not at all.

- As contemplation advances, God "gradually 'captures' the inner faculties. He first occupies the will and then the imagination and the intellect. This is why in the beginnings of infused prayer distractions are common: only the will is taken over. Later on, during deep absorptions and ecstatic prayer, these distractions cease."

- This contemplation is dark, meaning there are no images or concepts of God because we are learning how to know Him in a superior way that surpasses all reasoning or thought. "This prayer is neither vision nor locution nor feeling."

- We're unable to "figure out" or understand this kind of prayer. Dubay warns that trying to "dissect or analyze it by clear, concise ideas or concepts not only issues in frustration but also indicates a lack of understanding of what contemplation is."

- In the beginning, we may not be aware of all of these infusions, which are gentle and not long lasting, and may be punctuated with distractions. "But as the years go by, and if one's living of the Gospel keeps pace, what God gives increases not only in intensity but also in duration."

- Although these earliest signs of infused prayer seem normal and do not cause apprehension, later prayer gifts can be quite powerful and trigger fear as a first reaction. "It is not the beauty of the gift that begets the fear, but unfamiliarity with it. One wonders what it is and whence it comes."

- "Deepening communion with the indwelling Trinity brings with it a steadily progressive growth in holiness: humility, love, patience, purity, fortitude and all the virtues. So necessary is this trait that a gradual increase in day-to-day Gospel living is an indispensable sign of the genuineness of prayer."

The important thing to remember with these elements of contemplation is that there will always be an "ebb and flow" in intensity. For instance, we might experience "lost time" during prayer when we were unaware of anything at all — even of God – and yet afterward realized a deep interior peace, a clear indication that God has somehow touched us in prayer. The next day, our prayer might be as dry as sand. At another time, our prayer is so profound we're moved to tears.

This ebb and flow is typical of advancing prayer. "In all types of infused prayer, there are degrees of intensity, more or less, ebb and flow," Dubay writes.

This is God's way of keeping control while slowly detaching us from former methods of prayer. Once we learn how to let go and receive this mysterious infusion of God's presence, we begin to experience a kind of thrilling vulnerability, much like falling in love. Only with God, we're at the mercy of perfect and unconditional love, the likes of which cannot be found on earth except in that solitary place where heaven and earth truly meet – the union of the soul with God in prayer.

PITFALLS IN PRAYER

Confronting the Demons of Prayer

Prayer is one of the ripest areas for temptation, mostly because the devil knows if he can keep us from praying, he can keep us from God. This is why the demons that afflict our prayer life are particularly persistent.

As Segundo Galilea writes in his book, Temptation and Discernment: "If Christians are fervent, giving in to the 'demons' of prayer will leave them mediocre. If they are serving in the Church's ministry, they will become empty activists. If they are holy, they will cease being so. In every case, they will cease influencing the spread of the reign of God."

Let's look at the most common ways these demons attack our prayer life.

1. Not Being Sufficiently Motivated

This demon wants to keep our prayer shallow and superficial so that it can't become a dynamic force in our lives. One of the ways he does this is by keeping our motivation for prayer on the psychological level.

As Father Galilea explains: "Too many praying people have fallen into this temptation. Psychological needs, not faith, leads them to prayer. The psychological needs that lead us to prayer should not be undervalued – they can be a valuable aid – but they are insufficient: to feel devotion, to have desire and fervor, to cope with difficult moments that cause one to run to God, to obtain something, and so on. Once the psychological mood has changed, the motivation for prayer ceases."

We fight this demon by making sure that our prayer is motivated by faith, not just by our needs. Although God wants to help us in our needs, this cannot be the sole substance of our prayer life. We must learn to pray for God's sake and not just because we need something or because it makes us feel good.

2. Depersonalizing Prayer

This demon wants to reduce our prayer to a "religious experience," a "spiritual high," or an "altered state." It is all too common these days with the growth of New Age and eastern forms of prayer. As Father Galilea explains, this person prays to a "divinity" or a "supreme being" or a universal energy or some other seemingly powerful force.

Christian prayer, on the other hand, is essentially a personal relationship with God. We put ourselves into contact with a Person, not with a power or religious principle.

"This demon introduces a very concrete temptation," he explains. "When beginning to pray, some people neglect to be explicitly conscious of God personally present in the soul. For that reason, they do not enter into prayer and make profound contact with God."

No matter how much time it requires, we must always take the time to first put ourselves into the presence of God; otherwise, we run the risk of turning our prayer life into a religious experience that is largely centered on ourselves. "We practically ignore God as a person," Father writes. "We dialogue with ourselves rather than with God. We listen to ourselves, our plans, our good intentions, our needs, our faults, and sins, but do not listen to God."

3. Not Devoting Oneself Deeply to Prayer

This is another common attack by the devil – to tempt us to come to prayer physically, but with our minds focused elsewhere.

"We have one foot in prayer and the other outside. When the prayer time ends, we have prayed but we have not prayed, in that the quality of prayer has been poor."

Each time we pray, we must make a conscious choice for prayer, which can sometimes feel almost impossible, especially when we're in the middle of a hectic life with many concerns on our minds. Pray to the Holy Spirit, who has promised to help us pray as we ought, and ask for the grace to be fully present to God during your prayer time.

4. Putting Quantity Above Quality

Most of us have fallen victim to this demon at one time or another when we get into the habit of multiplying our devotions until we have little or no time left to spend in quiet conversation with God.

"Prayers worth and progress depend not so much on growth in quantity as on increase in quality. Less quantity of prayer but better quality is worth more than multiplying times of mediocre prayer (superficial, hurried, as one who fulfills a task)," Father Galilea writes.

The devil wants us to think that we're making progress in prayer because we're saying so many prayers, but that is not the case.

"This explains why so many people who...multiply prayer practices and piety do not change much in practical life and maintain grave errors. In some cases, the multiplication of practices constitutes a kind of idolatrous ritualism. They would benefit from allowing their moments of prayer, whether few or many, to be profound experiences of God."

5. *Neglecting Substantial Prayer Times*

The spiritual masters all warn us about this particular demon which encourages us to "pray when I get time" rather than to designating a set time every day for prayer. Praying-on-the-run never works because it gradually weakens and diminishes prayer until it disappears entirely.

"The spirit of prayer requires a framework of quality time dedicated exclusively to prayer," Father Galilea teaches.

Praying-on-the-fly just doesn't work because it gives us no time to quiet down and come into the presence of God. Without this, our prayer time becomes straggled and disconnected, comprised of 15-minutes here and 20-minutes there.

"This prayer life is highly precarious," Father warns. "All prayer life implies a firm dedication to prayer, with regular substantial times: that is, profound and therefore sufficiently prolonged periods of prayer. Otherwise, it is like wanting to be fed well by occasionally eating only a cracker or a piece of fruit, neglecting to eat a more substantial meal at least once a day. People who nourish themselves in that way will become weakened and anemic."

And so will their prayer life!

6. Not Putting Feelings in Their Proper Place

This is another very common temptation. First, it makes us place too much emphasis on our feelings, convincing us that our prayer is going well when we're experiencing consolations and that it is going badly if these feelings are absent.

The truth is the exact opposite. God often withdraws these favors as we advance in the spiritual life to wean us from coming to prayer in order to feel good rather than for Him.

If we fall to this temptation, we will cling to what we feel during prayer rather than to God, and eventually leave prayer entirely when it no longer gratifies our senses. This is a particularly dangerous temptation because one of the most common ways that the Lord matures us in prayer is to strip us of all sensible satisfaction in order to help us learn how to come to prayer for His sake and not our own.

Everyone goes through these dry spells from time to time in prayer which is why it's never too late to learn that if we're going to "accompany Christ in His splendor on Mount Tabor" we must be willing to accompany Him "in His aridity and agony in the garden of Gethsemane," Fr. Galilea writes.

The second temptation is the exact opposite – it makes us discard all feelings, thinking that because they are secondary, they don't matter.

"But this is not so," Father writes. "Sense perception and feelings, although not a permanent element in prayer, have a place in it. To underestimate their place is the temptation of angelism, since when we pray, we pray as people endowed with emotion and affect. ...Moreover, remember that particular types of temperaments – and everyone at some point in life – can make good use of affect and the senses."

Therefore, we should neither cling to, nor reject, feelings.

The bottom line is that no matter how many demons are plaguing our prayer, never stop praying!

As Teresa of Avila once wrote: "In spite of what wrong they who practice prayer do, they must not abandon prayer since it is the means by which they can remedy the situation. ... And if one perseveres, I trust then in the mercy of God, who never fails to repay anyone who has taken Him for a friend."

FOR JOURNALING

How do you practice the presence of God in your everyday life? Have you experienced any signs of advancing prayer? If so, which ones? Which "demons" are plaguing your prayer life?

Chapter Three

THIRD STAGE OF PRAYER
Spiritual Betrothal

When we reach this stage of prayer, God begins to do most of the work in prayer, "watering" our garden by means of a nearby stream or fountain. The profound silence of the Prayer of Quiet begins to give way to a much deeper absorption in God called the Prayer of Union or Spiritual Betrothal.

In this stage of prayer, not only is the will taken up by God, as was the case in the Prayer of Quiet, but also the imagination, memory and intellect. In the Prayer of Union, the person experiences a delight so deep and profound that St. Teresa of Avila describes the person as being "beside themselves" while experiencing it.

"The consolation, the sweetness, and the delight are incomparably greater than that experienced in the previous prayer. ...This prayer is a glorious foolishness, a heavenly madness . ...Often I had been as though bewildered and inebriated in this love...the soul would desire to cry out praises and is beside itself...it cannot bear so much joy..."

The tender, almost marital nature of this prayer, is why it is commonly referred to as a "betrothal." It is a union that takes place only in the interior of the soul and Teresa likens it to a "courtship" but one with "nothing that is not spiritual."

She explains that corporal union is different and that the spiritual joys and consolations give by the Lord "are a thousand leagues removed from those experienced in marriage. It is all a union of love with love, and its operations are entirely pure, and so delicate and gentle that there is no way of describing them."

But not all consolations mean we're entering into the prayer of union with God.

Understanding Consolations

We all receive supernatural favors from God during prayer even though we're not always aware of them. These favors are referred to as consolations and they are quite common, particularly those that can be felt by the senses which usually occur in those who are beginning a prayer life. Favors we do not feel are considered to be the most desirable. As the renowned spiritual master, Francois Fenelon once said, the consolations we can feel are "the dregs of grace."

But sometimes they're necessary, especially beginners in the spiritual life who are still very much attached to sensory delights and not yet resolved enough to stick to prayer when it doesn't feel good. God also uses consolations to soothe us if we're anxious or to revive our flagging spirits.

According to St. Teresa, authentic consolations from God will be accompanied by "the greatest peace and quietness and sweetness within ourselves." They will make us feel wonderful both inside and out.

There are three kinds of consolation in the spiritual order:

1. Sensible consolations are those that are felt chiefly in the senses. For example, they may come in the form of a feeling of fervor while participating in the Mass or other liturgical event. As such, they should not be discarded because they help to lead us to God and to desire what is good and holy.

2. The second kind of consolation, which is often the result of the first, is characterized by a delight in the exercise of the virtues, especially the theological virtues. St. Ignatius says that any increase in faith, hope, and charity, may be called a consolation. These consolations raise the soul above the sensible faculties where truth is perceived by faith alone, which brings about a kind of fervor of the will.

3. The third kind of consolation is more perfect than the first two because these affect the higher faculties of the soul, namely the intellect and the will. They consist of a special tranquility and peace of soul, and are the result of the firm determination of the will to live for God with entire confidence in His grace. It is present when, as St. Ignatius says, "the soul burns with the love of its Creator, and can no longer love any creature except for His sake." Even though a person may be suffering great affliction, they will be conscious of a deep happiness in the soul. This is considered to be the most perfect kind of consolation as well as being the rarest, and one experienced most often by souls who have reached a high level of perfection.

Thus, the first kind of consolation is said to belong to beginners in the way of perfection, the second to those who are making progress, and the third is said to belong to the perfect.

No matter what consolations God chooses to send us, Father de Caussade advises us to receive these gifts from God "with simplicity" and to "scrupulously abstain from counteracting His designs by fussy inquiries and indiscreet curiosity."

We should remain indifferent even in the opposite situation, when God chooses to withdraw these consolations from our prayer life, which He will do on occasion, and for sometimes long periods of time.

For our part, we should strive to receive only the consolations God wishes to send us – no more and no less.

In the prayer of union, the kind of consolations God sends us are "a thousand leagues removed from those experienced in marriage," St. Teresa describes.

"It is all a union of love with love, and its operations are entirely pure, and so delicate and gentle that there is no way of describing them."

The length of this absorption is brief, never longer than a half hour, but it is very intense and accompanied by a profound certainty that it comes from God. This makes the experience indelible, St. Teresa says. Even years later, a person will remember the exact time and circumstances in which this absorption occurred.

However, during this prayer, one understands nothing of the favor being granted. St. Teresa says it is like being struck blind and dumb, like St. Paul at his conversion. During this prayer, "the intellect is as though in awe," she says. "The will loves more than it understands, but it doesn't understand in a describable way whether it loves or what it does; there is no memory at all, in my opinion, nor any thought."

The results of this prayer are even more intense. “In this profound absorption, one emerges with a consuming desire to praise God and to die a thousand deaths for His sake,” Fr. Dubay explains.

“There are likewise vehement yearnings for penance and solitude together with keen longings that everyone would come to know this God of unspeakable bounty. This person, having tasted so deeply of the very best, understandably is satisfied now with nothing this world has to offer, sets no store by what can be seen or touched and finds no rest in anything finite.”

This doesn’t mean the soul loses its peace, however. Instead, the person enjoys a calm so profound that not even severe trials can disturb it. The only thing that bothers this soul is that too few people are willing to love and serve God.

“This grief is infused and not simply the result of our meditations,” Fr. Dubay writes. “It reaches so deeply into one’s being that it ‘seems to tear it to pieces and grind it to powder.’”

But beware! These and other experiences in advanced stages of prayer have a downside. The delights experienced are hard to resist, and if one is not vigilant and constantly working to develop themselves in humility, it’s much too easy to start striving after these favors.

St. Teresa explicitly warns about submitting to this temptation and gives three very good reasons why we should not be concerned with favors: 1) because it is essential that we love God without any motive of self-interest; 2) because it is a sign of a lack of humility to think we ought to get them, and 3) because the only true preparation to receive these favors is the desire to suffer in imitation of Christ.

Now more than ever the soul must live the Gospel without compromise. From the soul who reaches this stage of prayer, "...The Lord asks only two things," Teresa writes, "love for His majesty and love for our neighbor. It is for these two virtues that we must strive and if we attain them perfectly we are doing His will and so shall be united with Him."

Even though the Lord may choose to favor a soul with the ecstatic prayer of union, this doesn't matter nearly as much as an authentic living of the Gospel.

"When I see people very diligently trying to discover what kind of prayer they are experiencing and so completely wrapped up in their prayers that they seem afraid to stir or to indulge in a moment's thought lest they should lose the slightest degree of tenderness...which they have been feeling, I realize how little they understand of the road to the attainment of union," Teresa writes. "They think that the whole thing consists in this. But no. . . what the Lord desires is works."

Experiencing God in Prayer

Human weakness makes it very difficult to keep the experience of God in its proper place, especially when those experiences are intense and profound. This is an area about which most people are very curious. What does it feel like to come into contact with God? Is it frightening, overwhelming, thrilling?

If you answered "none of the above," you're correct, but not because experiences of God are rare. God's touch is pure spirit and in the early stages of our spiritual life, when we're still very worldly and sense-oriented, we are barely able to distinguish the Divine touch.

But once we begin to advance in prayer and virtue, there are no words to describe what a person experiences during direct contact with the Living God.

"When God gives someone the unspeakable experience of Himself in contemplative immersion, He leaves no stone unturned," writes Father Dubay.

Relying on the expertise of St. Teresa and St. John of the Cross, Fr. Dubay gives us a sound set of guidelines for determining the various ways that man can experience God in prayer at the ordinary level rather than the extraordinary which occurs in more advanced levels of prayer. These latter experiences will be discussed later in this study.

It's important to understand that "contact with God is not immediately perceptible to the senses," Fr. Dubay teaches. "Nothing bodily or material is felt, seen or heard. This is contrary to what almost everyone mutually assumes, namely, that emotions run high in a meeting with the Lord. ...The contact itself is of the spiritual order, an order beyond sense phenomena."

Especially in the beginning, Dubay writes, these divine touches are "delicate, wordless and imageless. These perceptions are received, that is, not produced by our thought processes."

In other words, God doesn't want to scare us to death so these touches are gentle at first. Ever so gradually, He helps us become accustomed to the "feel" of Him.

For instance, we may simply feel "drawn" to prayer, or to a sudden loving awareness of God that occurs without any effort on our part. Many people who make a practice of praying in the Presence of the Eucharist say that they feel an inexplicable calm after their holy hour, even though nothing all that dramatic seemed to have taken place during the hour.

These are contacts with God.

But how do we know if what we're feeling is authentic? For that matter, how can we be sure that the "voice" we're hearing is really coming from God.

Discerning God's Voice in Prayer

Many of us have had experiences when we were sure God had just spoken to us. But is this even possible? Does God really speak to average people like us?

Of course!

Father Benedict Groeschel writes in his book, *A Still Small Voice*, "Private revelation is possible for the same reasons that public revelation is possible. The Divine Being can and does communicate with limited created beings."

God does speak to us, but the limitations of our humanness make private revelation far from an exact science. Delusion is so possible, in fact, that one of the Church's most renowned masters of the mystical life, St. John of the Cross, advises us to completely ignore anything we might hear or see in prayer, even if we see the Lord God Himself and all the saints with Him. Why? Because we can get to heaven on faith alone, without a single vision or even one blessed peep from the Lord.

However, everyone who prays can benefit from the practical guidelines of the Church and her saints on the subject of public and private revelation.

According to *The Catechism of the Catholic Church*, "It is not the role (of private revelations) to improve or complete Christ's definitive (public) revelation, but to help one live more fully by it in a certain period of history" (*CCC* 67). In other words, as St. John of the Cross says, private revelation is not really necessary, although it can be helpful to us in applying the Gospel to our everyday lives.

So how might God reveal Himself to us in the privacy of prayer? In her book, *The Interior Castle*, St. Teresa of Avila goes into great detail about the three types of utterances, or locutions, in which God may communicate with us:

Corporeal locutions are those actually heard by the physical power of hearing, which are very rare and, therefore, highly suspect. The devil is more than capable of speaking to us and can fool even the most adept soul. Teresa's recommendation is to ignore these messages because even if they are authentic, they will return much stronger and we will have lost nothing.

Imaginary locutions, the second type, are those referring to the imaginative faculty which receives the same kind of impression it would have received had it heard words.

Intellectual locutions, the third type, are considered the most reliable. In this type, God imprints what He is about to say in the depth of the spirit, without the use of a voice or sounds. It is often described as an "infusion of knowledge," or a sudden clear understanding of some subject or situation. This may seem like a simple enough explanation of how God communicates with souls, but there are many hidden complexities that must be addressed.

St. Teresa of Avila gives us much practical advice on how to discern authentic communication from God:

First, she teaches that unless what we hear in prayer agrees with Scripture, we should "take no more notice of it than you would if it came from the devil himself."

Second, the words will have a power and authority both in themselves and in the actions which follow them. For instance, St. Teresa gives the example of a soul who is experiencing all kinds of disturbances, who receives the impression of a single statement, "Be not troubled" and is instantly calmed.

Third, one will experience "a great tranquility that dwells in the soul and makes it peaceful and devoutly recollected." Peace, joy, and confidence are all effects that accompany communications from God.

If locutions are coming from our own imagination, none of these signs occur, nor will we feel the kind of deep certainty, peace or interior consolation that accompanies God's communications. We can make ourselves hear what we want and be momentarily soothed, but it won't last.

In fact, God's communications have such a profound impact, a soul will find it almost impossible to experience the same disturbances it had before.

It is important to note here that critical, antagonistic, suspicious, anxious and fearful thoughts are signs of the devil's activity and should be banished the instant they are recognized. When locutions come from the devil, although he might be able to pronounce the words (thoughts) with undeniable clarity, he will not be able to counterfeit these peaceful "effects" of God's words, only restlessness and turmoil.

Another important sign of an authentic communication from God is that the words do not vanish from memory for a very long time. "Some indeed never vanish at all," St. Teresa writes.

"Words which we hear on earth, however weighty and learned they may be – we do not bear so deeply engraved upon our memory, nor, if they refer to the future, do we give credence to them as we do to these locutions. For these last impress us by their complete certainty ... although sometimes they seem quite impossible of fulfillment . . .yet within the soul itself there is a certainty which cannot be overcome."

It's easy to pray about something that makes us anxious, such as if our mortgage will be approved or a medical test will prove normal, and to "imagine" God telling us the result we want to hear. This is just human nature.

But when a prophetic word from God is authentic, no matter what happens in reality, the person will not be able to shake the feeling that the words they heard will happen eventually, in spite of what might be happening at the present moment.

Even if years go by and a soul begins to doubt what was heard, St. Teresa writes, "There still remains within it a living spark of conviction that it will come true." She describes this spark of conviction as being so tenacious that even if we wished to stop believing in what we heard, we could not do it.

She goes on to say that authentic communications are always very clear. "Even if it consists of a long exhortation, the hearer notices the omission of a single syllable, as well as the phraseology which is used." In locutions created by the imagination, the words are less distinct, like something heard in a half-dream.

Particularly in the case of intellectual locutions, "... often the soul has not been thinking of what it hears, I mean that the voice (insight) comes unexpectedly....Often it refers to things which one never thought would or could happen, so that the imagination could not possibly have invented them."

A person cannot be deceived about things it never desired or even knew about!

She also teaches that in genuine locutions, the soul seems to be hearing something, but in locutions contrived by the imagination, "someone seems to be composing bit by bit what the soul wishes to hear."

Also in a genuine locution, a single word (insight) can contain a world of meaning, such as the natural understanding could not have managed on its own.

More important than all of these clues is how much humility is inspired within us by this communication from God.

Teresa explains, "it is quite certain that the greater the favor the soul receives, the less by far it esteems itself, the more keenly it remembers its sins, the more forgetful it is of its own interest, the more fervent are the efforts of its will in seeking nothing but the honor of God rather than being mindful of its own profit...and its certainty that it has never deserved these favors, but only hell."

In other words, authentic communication with God produces personal, even heroic goodness, and a level of virtue that is beyond human capability.

Advanced Experiences

And then there are the advanced experiences which occur when these gentle contacts increase in intensity and duration. Our contact with God on the spiritual level may begin to overflow into the senses and emotions and feel more like an ardent yearning or a burning thirst for God.

St. John of the Cross describes how intense these experiences can get. "The unction of the Holy Spirit overflows into the body...All the members and bones and marrow rejoice...with a feeling of great delight and glory, even in the outermost joints of the hands and feet."

St. Teresa of Avila called these experiences, "a heavenly madness...a glorious foolishness."

Believe it or not, this kid of burning love and intense inner light is considered ordinary by theologians or, as Dubay writes, "within the scope of God's usual dealing in salvation history."

He goes on to say that "Anyone who has done extensive spiritual direction has probably met a number of completely normal men and women (and sometimes even small children) who have been suddenly swept off their feet by an unspeakable inner flooding of light, and/or love, and/or delight whose origin can be nothing other than God Himself."

Impulses/Touches

An impulse is a desire that frequently comes upon the soul quite suddenly and without any preceding prayer. During this impulse, God will give the person a secret knowledge of Himself. This experience is so keen and absorbing that, as St. Teresa once described, a person would feel no pain "even if they were being cut to pieces."

Raptures/Ecstasies

A rapture or ecstasy, between which there are only accidental differences, occurs when a person experiences a deep union with God and is completely absorbed in Him. During this absorption, God communicates great things to them, although they are frequently unable to describe them in human terms after the rapture ceases. A person can fluctuate in and out of this state for several hours. Although their senses are almost entirely shut down, they are sometimes able to distinguish sounds as if from far away.

St. Teresa of Avila once described the body in a rapture to be "as dead, unable to move." It remains in whatever position it was when the rapture occurred; sitting or standing, eyes open or closed. One of the most famous cases of a rapture occurred to St. Catherine of Siena who was stirring a pot of soup over an open fire when God swept her up into Himself. In proof of His exquisite thoughtfulness was the fact that when St. Catherine returned to herself, neither she nor the family's dinner was burned!

Father Dubay points out that this kind of ecstatic prayer is not to be feared. In fact, it actually improves physical health, making a person feel rejuvenated, mentally, physically and spiritually.

Transports/Flights of Spirit

Unlike raptures that occur gradually, transports and flights of spirit are much more sudden. A person feels as if their soul has left their body, and that they were taken into another world where they were shown great things by God. A deep peace accompanies these experiences and will sometimes last for days afterward.

As the spiritual masters teach, the person who receives these experiences is one who has become totally surrendered to God and who has remained faithful during many seasons of testing. But these are not strange or marginal people. Rather, these souls are living at maximum capacity, full of vitality and energy, while enjoying that perfect peace of soul known only to those who have died to all but Christ.

PITFALLS IN PRAYER

Aridity & Dryness

As ecstatic as prayer can be in these stages, aridity and dryness can still occur. No one escapes these two banes of prayer which can be painful and disturbing. Where once our prayer was filled with joy, all of a sudden the lights go out and we're barely able to string together two good thoughts. We are then assailed by all kinds of fears. Have we stopped loving God? Is He angry at us for something, perhaps some unconfessed sin?

Dryness is especially difficult to understand when it appears in the wake of prayer that used to be so full of joy and consolation. Time never passed so quickly as when we were alone with God. And then, all of a sudden, the pleasure disappears. Prayer becomes empty, dry, without even a drop of fervor.

The Way to Spiritual Maturity

If this has happened to you, you may have wondered at the time – what's going on? This question can be answered in two words – a lot. The process of moving closer to God involves learning how to let go of pleasant feelings in prayer. In fact, difficult prayer is precisely what distinguishes the spiritually mature from the beginner.

Father Thomas Dubay writes in *Fire Within*, "Fidelity in the midst of aridity proves that we are seeking God and not merely our own satisfaction."

Jesus, the greatest spiritual Master of all, said, "God is spirit and those who worship Him must worship in Spirit and in truth" (Jn. 4:24). A spirit does not have a body; therefore, it does not have feelings. Perhaps this is why Father de Caussade wrote, "Feelings are the dregs of grace." Prayer without feelings of sweetness is normally purer and more pleasing to God. "For such is the way of pure spirit and of pure love that asks nothing for itself."

Other Causes of Dry Prayer

However, there could be other causes of dryness, such as physical or emotional disturbances, illness, fatigue, depression, troublesome preoccupations or excessive work. Some of these conditions may last a long time. St. Teresa of Avila advises those who are long-suffering in this manner to "... Turn to vocal prayer, or reading, or colloquies with God, but never fail to consecrate to prayer the time set apart for it." In other words, we should stick to our normal prayer habits as if nothing was wrong.

Father Gabriel of St. Mary Magdalen describes a more serious cause of dryness in prayer. He writes in *Divine Intimacy*, "Sometimes it is the result of infidelity on the part of those who, little by little, have become lax, allowing themselves many slight satisfactions and pleasures and giving in to their curiosity, selfishness or pride."

As St. Teresa of Avila taught, "Prayer cannot be accompanied by self-indulgence."

Father Dubay advises beginners not to pine after lost consolations but to keep moving. "The beginner especially needs to get on with solid virtue and generous suffering, for it 'rains manna' later. The divine downpour can only occur when the way is cleared by the unspectacular practice of self-denial, obedience, humility and patience."

He calls empty prayer "indispensable" for burning away many imperfections such as impatience, worldly inclinations, vanities and laxness.

The time has come to pick up our cross and follow Christ, and we do this by accepting rather than resisting dry devotion. If we do this, we will give ourselves a great opportunity to acquire humility. What a vivid experience of our ineptness! The Little Flower used these experiences to remind herself of how little she was capable of doing for God. Father Dubay echoes her sentiments when he writes: "We learn concretely what we may have thus far understood only in theory, that without God we can do nothing. Thus we are grounded in a realistic humility so that later favors will not puff us up."

For all of us who are struggling through periods of dryness in prayer, it will certainly help us to keep these words of Father Gabriel in the forefront of our minds: "One who, in order to please God, perseveres in prayer although he finds no consolation in it, but rather even repugnance, gives Him a beautiful proof of true love."

FOR JOURNALING

Is your prayer full of consolations, as dry as a desert, or a little of both? How would you describe your experiences of God in prayer? Have you ever had an experience in prayer that you don't understand? How does God typically talk to you? Describe it here.

Chapter Four

FOURTH STAGE OF PRAYER
Transforming Union

In the fourth stage of prayer, the garden of the soul is now being watered directly by God who is sending it a soft soaking rain of delights along with great fires of love. The soul has undergone two major stages of purification – the "night of the Senses" and, much later, the "night of the soul." It has finally reached the summit of spiritual perfection and the purpose of its creation – the achievement of total union with God. The soul now lives for God alone, is well advanced in God-centeredness and in living the Gospel message.

At this point, the ecstatic absorptions of the third stage of prayer gradually begin to give way to ever deeper tastes of the divine elixir. The spiritual betrothal of the third stage of prayer, which takes place during the prayer of union, is now ready to advance to its final stage which is known as the prayer of transforming union or spiritual marriage.

According to St. Teresa of Avila, what the soul experiences during this marriage is beyond the scope of human language. In her case, it occurred just after she received communion one day and began when the Lord favored her with a vision unlike any other she had ever experienced.

"The Lord appeared in the center of the soul, not through an imaginary but through an intellectual vision, just as He appeared to the Apostles, without entering through the door...This instantaneous communication of God to the soul is so great a secret and so sublime a favor and such delight is felt by the soul that I do not know with what to compare it, beyond saying that the Lord is pleased to manifest to the soul...the glory that is in heaven, in a more sublime manner than is possible through any vision or spiritual consolation."

Nothing was seen with the eyes or the imagination, but was more like a sudden infusion of knowledge. It's as if God removes the "scales from the eyes of the soul" and allows it to "see" the Blessed Trinity.

Through a special kind of illumination, St. Tersea writes, the soul "sees these three Persons individually, and yet, with a wonderful kind of knowledge which is given to it, the soul realizes that...all these three Persons are one Substance, and one Power, and one Knowledge, and one God alone; so that what we hold by faith, the soul may be said here to grasp by sight, although nothing is seen by the eyes, either of the body or of the soul."

After this mysterious union, the soul receives a whole new awareness of the indwelling Trinity. Unlike spiritual betrothal, when God and the soul would unite and then separate in the prayer of union, in spiritual marriage they become one on a permanent basis.

Teresa wrote that no matter how numerous were her trials and business worries, the essential part of her soul was permanently fixed in this placid dwelling place. She once described herself as feeling "divided" because her soul could remain in perfect peace even while life was erupting as usual all around her. Sometimes she would even grumble that her soul was "doing nothing but enjoying itself" while she was left with all the trials of life.

This description should dismantle any notions that the person who reaches this stage of prayer does nothing but kneel in prayer and stare at the sky all day. Quite the contrary. These people are more alive than any of us.

"It would be a mistake to conclude that this person... is inert or living in a marginal manner," Father Dubay writes. "Inner life and vitality are increased...this is supreme living."

By making this incredible journey into the heart of God, they have achieved the ultimate purpose in life and have become precisely the person they were created to be.

Now that you've had a glimpse of the incredible mystical journey we call "prayer," it's important to remember that infused prayer is a gift from God and can never be learned from a book or acquired through the mastering of techniques such as those taught in transcendental meditation and Centering Prayer. It is something wholly "received." The most we can do is to prepare for it by creating within ourselves the right disposition to receive it.

"Progress in the prayer life is not measured chronologically by the number of years one has lived the religions life or practiced meditation," Father Dubay writes. "Growth is determined first of all by readiness and generosity. When these are present in a high degree, God gives much in a short time."

But how can we "average" folks ever hope to reach this level of prayer?

By doing precisely what the saints did – they learned how to rely on God and not themselves.

As simple as this might sound, the ability to rely on God rather than self is considered to be one of the most important lessons we can learn.

As Father J. P. de Caussaude sums up so succinctly: " . . .(C)omplete distrust of self combined with utter trust in Him. . . are the two great props of the spiritual life."

No one exemplified this truth better than St. Therese of Lisieux who described this concept with her trademark simplicity in a letter she wrote to her sister Celine in 1889:

"We would like never to fall. What an illusion! What does it matter, my Jesus, if I fall at every moment? I come to recognize by it how weak I am and that is gain for me. You see by that how little I am able to do and You will be more likely to carry me in your arms. If you do not do so, it is because you like to see me prostrate on the ground. Well, then, I am not going to worry, but I will always stretch out my suppliant arms toward You with great love. I cannot believe You would abandon me."

St. Therese was fully aware of both the infinite greatness and goodness of God and her own weakness and tendency to evil. Basing one's spiritual life on the combination of these two qualities became the beloved Little Way of Spiritual Childhood that has led millions to a closer walk with Jesus.

This sounds simpler than it is. Our pride does everything in its power to prevent us from seeing ourselves for who we really are.

"For although in ourselves we are nothing, we are too apt to overestimate our own abilities and to conclude falsely that we are of some importance," writes Dom Lorenzo Scupoli in his masterpiece, *The Spiritual Combat.* "This vice springs from the corruption of our nature. But the more natural a thing is, the more difficult it is to be discovered."

In other words, we have a tendency to believe that we're trusting in God and not ourselves but may be overlooking a million ways in which we're doing just the opposite.

For instance, how many times have we struggled to overcome a temptation to overeat, vent on a co-worker, watch prurient shows or movies, only to fall time and time again? We confess these recurring sins every month, determined to do better, but even with our best intentions, we keep falling.

Too much trust in ourselves and not enough awareness of our own dependence on God may be the culprit behind these repeated failures. Of course, we have to do our best to overcome these temptations, but we may be so focused on fixing it ourselves that we've neglected to ask God for His help.

"This distrust of our own strength is a gift from Heaven, bestowed by God on those He loves," Father Scupoli writes. "It is granted sometimes through his holy inspiration, sometimes through severe afflictions, or almost insurmountable temptations, and other ways which are unknown to us."

The easiest way to see how much we distrust ourselves is to look at how we react to a fall, Father Scupoli writes. "If he yields to anger and despairs of advancing in the way of virtue, it is evident that he placed his confidence in himself and not in God. The greater the anxiety and despondence, the greater is the certainty of his guilt."

Much like Saint Therese exemplified in her letter to Celine, when a person has a deep distrust of himself and great confidence in God, they are not at all surprised when they commit a fault. They correctly attribute what has happened to their own weakness and lack of confidence in God, repent of their mistake, then run straight to Jesus for help.

Asking for a "sign" can be another way of believing we're trusting in God and not ourselves. Although signs are sometimes needed to build up our faith, when God chooses not to give them, do we bow our head in surrender to His will or abandon all hope?

Father Scupoli recommends four means of acquiring distrust of self and trust in God:

First, we should meditate upon our own weakness, not in a morbid way, but with a calm realization that without divine assistance, we cannot accomplish anything but sin.

Second, we must beg God for this virtue. "Let us begin by acknowledging not only that we do not possess it, but that of ourselves we are utterly incapable of acquiring it." But we must be careful to ask with a firm confidence that we will indeed be heard "if we patiently await the effect of our prayer and persevere in it as long as it pleases Divine Providence."

Third, we must gradually accustom ourselves to distrust our own self, to dread the illusions of our mind, our tendency to sin and the number of temptations that continually assault us. We should calmly face this reality, not to breathe fear into ourselves, but to push us ever closer to God, our only hope.

Fourth, when we commit a fault, we should examine our conscience in order to discover where we're most vulnerable. "God permits us to fall only that we may gain a deeper insight into ourselves, that we may learn to despise ourselves as wretched creatures... Without this we cannot hope to obtain distrust of self which is rooted in humility and the knowledge of our own weakness."

PITFALLS IN PRAYER

Inordinate Attachments

"Blessed are the pure of heart, for they shall see God."

This is one of the most important beatitudes for those who wish to advance in prayer because it requires the emptying of our hearts of all that could stand between God and us.

To be pure of heart means not only the absence of sin, but also the absence of the slightest earthly affection. This is an important definition for those of us who are stumbling toward perfection, because we tend to be on the lookout for sin much more than the latter category of earthly affection. But it's those earthly affections – also known as attachments – that can be a serious impediment in our quest for intimacy with God in prayer.

Attachments, like all sin and imperfection, have a clouding effect on the soul. St. John of the Cross compares the presence of attachments to the smattering of dirt on a clean window. Instead of seeing the full radiance of the sun, we're allowing only a small glow to get through because our windows are smeared with too many worldly concerns – job, family, possessions, inter-personal relationships. Letting go of these concerns doesn't mean forsaking family and friends or being careless on the job – it means learning how to care for them for God's sake and not our own.

As Father Gabriel writes in his book, *Divine Intimacy*, "God wishes us to love ourselves, as well as all created things, in the measure assigned by Him, with a view to His pleasure and not to our own selfish satisfaction." This is also what St. Paul meant when he advised that whatever we eat or drink, or whatever else we do, we should do it all for the glory of God.

If we don't follow this advice, these things can become "little gods" to which we are constantly made to answer. They are forever ordering us around, demanding satisfaction, which inadvertently saps our mental, physical and spiritual energy.

How do we know if we're suffering from an inordinate attachment?

St. John of the Cross gives us three signs:

1. ***The first sign is if the activity or thing is diverted from the purpose God intends for it.*** For example, if one uses the tongue to lie in order to get ahead on the job, this shows an inordinate attachment to one's own gain, not to the glory of God.

2. ***The second sign is an excess of use.*** Father Dubay writes: "As soon as we go too far in eating, drinking, recreating, speaking, or working, we show that there is something disordered in our activity. We cannot honestly direct to the glory of God what is in excess of

what He wills." This can mean buying more clothes that we need, working more than necessary, traveling more extensively than we ought. These are some of the more obvious signs of inordinate attachment, but there are many less recognizable forms, such as being too attached to our own opinion or reputation, to little vanities and comforts, to unrestrained curiosity and idle chatter.

3. ***The third sign is making the means into an end.*** For instance, when we engage in idle talk just for the sake of talking, or eat just for the sake of eating, etc.

Father Gabriel explains that "The will of the soul which freely assents to these failings, slight though they be, is stained by this opposition to the will of God; for this reason a perfect union cannot exist between its will and God's."

Selfish clinging to things or creatures focuses too much attention on ourselves rather than on God, thus drawing us away from Him. It prevents us from preferring what pleases God to what pleases ourselves. Most of the distractions we suffer in prayer are due to these disordered concerns and desires. Our hearts remain divided between love of God and love of mammon. Prayer too often feels more like a tug-of-war than a quiet visit to our eternal Fatherland.

A further concern is that disordered attachments almost always give rise to venial sins, or at least to deliberate imperfections when we willingly yield to them, even though it may be only in matters of the slightest importance. Being too concerned about our reputation can lead us into sins of vanity, envy, or avarice. Idle chatter is too often the doorway to gossip or at least the wasting of time. Being too impressed with our own opinions can make us uncharitable and argumentative. Requiring too much comfort and luxury can make us lazy and morally weak.

We too often brush off these weaknesses with, "I'm only human," but the truth is, we're not "only human" beings. We're spiritual beings too, and just like over-indulging in severe penances and mortifications can damage our physical health, so can consenting to worldly attachments damage our spiritual health.

But before we embark on a serious plan of detachment, we must seek God's help in prayer. This is an important first step because, as Father Dubay writes, "While detachment furthers prayer, prayer furthers attachment. Growth in prayer gives us the knowledge of what is and what is not really important in life. . . "

It is only when we start letting go of our selfish satisfactions and pursuits that we realized how much our clinging to inconsequential things deprived us of the spiritual joy and calm God meant for us to have. The pain of breaking an attachment or two suddenly seems like nothing compared to the hardship those appetites were imposing upon us every day of our lives.

FOR JOURNALING

What was your reaction when you read about the prayer of transforming union? Did it surprise you, intrigue you, or make you feel as if it could never be possible for you? How often do you ask God for help in the course of a day? Make a note of what occasions caused you to seek His aid. What attachments are you clinging to today – people, possessions, reputation, schedule? Make a list and pray for God's help in "cutting the cord" that binds you to each one.

Bibliography

Barbaric, Slavko, *Pray with the Heart.* (Steubenville, Ohio. *Franciscan University Press*, 1992)

Clark, John, *The Story of a Soul: The Autobiography of St. Therese of Lisieux.* (Washington, DC. *ICS Publications*, 1972)

DeCaussade, Jean-Pierre, *Self-Abandonment to Divine Providence.* (Rockford, Ill. *Tan Books and Publishers*, 1987)

Scupoli, Dom Lorenzo, *The Spiritual Combat and a Treatise on Peace of Soul* (Rockford, Ill. *Tan Books and Publishers*, 1990)

Drexelius, Jeremiah, *Heliotropium: Conformity of the Human Will to the Divine* (Rockford, Ill. *Tan Books and Publishers*, 1984)

Dubay, Thomas, *Fire Within: St. Teresa of Avila, St. John of the Cross, and the Gospel – On Prayer* (San Francisco, Ca. *Ignatius Press*, 1989)

Gabriel of St. Mary Magdalen, *Divine Intimacy: Meditations on the Interior Life for Every Day of the Liturgical Year* (Rockford, Ill. *Tan Books and Publishers*, 1996)

Groeschel, Benedict J., *Listening at Prayer* (Mahwah, NJ. *Paulist Press*, 1984)

Hampsch, John, *Speak Up Lord, I Can't Hear You* (Santa Barbara, Ca. *Queenship Publishing*, 2000)

Jamart, Francois, *The Complete Spiritual Doctrine of St. Therese of Lisieux* (New York, NY. *Alba House*, 1961)

Johnston, William, *Silent Music: The Science of Meditation* (New York, NY. *Harper & Rowe Publishers, Inc.*, 1974)

Kavanaugh, Kieran, *The Way of Perfection: Study Edition* (Washington, DC. *ICS Publications*, 2000)

Kavanaugh, Kieran & Rodriguez, Otilio , *The Collected Works of St. John of the Cross* (Washington, DC. *ICS Publications,* 1991)

Lawrence of the Resurrection, *The Practice of the Presence of God* (New Kensington, Pa. *Whitaker House,* 1982)

Peers, E. Allison, *The Life of Teresa of Jesus* (Garden City, NY. *Image Books*, 1960)

Peers, E. Allison, *The Interior Castle* (Garden City, NY. *Image Books*, 1960)

Poulan, R.P. Aug. *The Graces of Interior Prayer* (Montana. *Kessinger Publishing Company*, 1910)

Welcome to Carmel (Hubertus, Wisc., *Teresian Charism Press*, 1998)

Wilkinson, Peggy, *Finding the Mystic Within You* (Washington, DC. *ICS Publications*, 1986)

About the Catholic Life Institute

The Catholic Life Institute, acting under the patronage of the Immaculate Heart of Mary and Our Lady of Mount Carmel, is a lay-run apostolate devoted to infusing the world with the truth and splendor of the Catholic mystical tradition as revealed by the Carmelite saints and Doctors of the Church.

The Institute was founded by members of the Immaculate Heart of Mary Chapter of Discalced Secular Carmelites from Willow Grove, Pennsylvania to introduce Carmelite spirituality and authentic Catholic contemplation to the faithful. Our programs include courses on Teresian prayer, the interior life, the Little Way of Spiritual Childhood as taught by St. Therese of Lisieux, and spiritual warfare.

Our programs are presented by Susan Brinkmann, OCDS, an award-winning Catholic journalist who serves as the Director of Communications and New Age research for Women of Grace. She is the author of several books and is a frequent guest on EWTN. Her areas of expertise are in Carmelite prayer and spirituality, the New Age, and the occult.

The Catholic Life Institute Press is our newest addition and is used to publish our workbooks and other publications. In addition to our own books, the Institute also provides a wide collection of Church-approved Catholic books at discounted prices.

Our courses, books, retreats, and seminars are faithful to the Magisterium and completely free of New Age components.

Visit www.freeandfaithful.com for more information.

Made in the USA
Middletown, DE
17 September 2022